The #getoutofyourownwaychallenge allowed me to see patterns that had eluded me for a while. The questions are phrased in a way that I normally wouldn't ask on my own and thus gave me answers that I really had to sit with and process. New angles shine new light!
SÌNE MÀIRI NI AILPIN

Never ask the cards a question you're not ready to hear the answer to! Especially 31 times in a row! If you're ready to engage in shadow work around your creativity and passion, Mariëlle S. Smith's #getoutofyourownway tarot challenge is a wonderful place to start. The questions and the timeline really dug into who I was as a writer and then more specifically, why and what I am writing about now. Each day is designed to take you back again and again to the core of an issue. I heartily recommend recording the answers after each session and then coming back at the end of the challenge and journal through the cards one more time, to see the patterns. Don't skip days and don't double up. The time between readings is important and what comes up might astonish you. I certainly didn't expect to have so many repeated cards in different positions, all angling back at the same place. The Universe seems to enjoy slamming the hammer home, so to speak, until we get the message. As Mariëlle said on one of my Instagram posts, 'Let the bitch slapping continue!' I certainly will. And I look forward to more of Mariëlle S. Smith's spreads.
BETHANY TUCKER

It seems that the constellation of these questions hit the nail on the head. Mariëlle S. Smith's spreads brings a certain order to the creative process, pointing out rooms for improvement as well as showing the fundaments. No foggy predictions here, but a No Bullshit approach— which I think is how tarot should be approached.
NIELS VONBERG

COPYRIGHT © 2019 BY M.S. WORDSMITH

ALL PHOTOGRAPHS COPYRIGHT © 2019 BY ANDRI HADJIPOLY

ALL RIGHTS RESERVED.

NO PART OF THIS BOOK MAY BE REPRODUCED IN ANY FORM OR BY ANY ELECTRONIC OR MECHANICAL MEANS, INCLUDING INFORMATION STORAGE AND RETRIEVAL SYSTEMS, WITHOUT WRITTEN CONSENT OF THE COPYRIGHT HOLDER, EXCEPT FOR THE USE OF BRIEF QUOTATIONS IN A BOOK REVIEW.

GET OUT OF YOUR OWN WAY

ABOUT ME

I'm a coach for writers and other creatives, an editor, writer, intuitive healer, and custom retreat organiser. Born in the Netherlands and raised by my Dutch mother and Scottish expat father, I moved to the island of Cyprus in February 2019.

The thing about being somewhere new is that it sheds a different light on your life. Your mind opens up to other perspectives, and you find yourself brimming with exciting new plans and ideas. Or, as was my case, old plans and ideas that you never took seriously suddenly start to demand your attention.

Organising a tarot challenge was a scary step for me. Not just because it was something I'd never done before; I've always tried to keep the spiritual out of my work. I say 'tried' because quite a few of the clients I've attracted over the past years, and the work they brought with them, actually forced me to merge my professional background with my spiritual interests.

Some hired me to edit or translate their holistic books, others came to me for coaching and were struggling in a way that needed a broader approach. And then there is the fact that so many writers and other creatives I know seem to be addicted to their crystals, essential oils, cards, meditation, and what nots.

Over the past year, I've switched gears and gradually allowed the spiritual to enter my work space. This book is one of its many manifestations. It goes without saying that I hope you'll enjoy it, and get from it everything you need.

Mariëlle S. Smith

FOREWORD

Welcome to *Get Out of Your Own Way*, the 31-day tarot challenge to get writers and other creatives back on track and in touch with their muses!

Get Out of Your Own Way: A 31-Day Tarot Challenge for Writers and Other Creatives is for every creative entrepreneur who is ready to (re)connect to their intuition to learn more about their creative processes and obstacles and figure out what their soul calls for them to create right now.

How does it work?

Every day comes with its own spread. Some days it's one question asking for one card, other days the question is layered or in need of more cards. There will be times when you feel the need to draw more cards than the question indicates, and you should always follow your intuition in those cases.

The challenge works best if you note your results and interpretations down and keep them by your side as you go through the different questions. The days build upon each other and will ask you to return to previous draws. Some cards might even show up multiple times, and reflecting on those earlier moments will help you peel away the different layers and go that much deeper.

Although I created this challenge with my favourite tarot deck in mind, there is no reason why you shouldn't use any other means of divination as you go through it. Pick your favourite oracle deck or set of angel cards, use your crystals or your runes. Whatever speaks to you, go with that. If you want to mix it up during the challenge, do it. It's all good. It's your challenge, after all.

DAY 1

WHAT ARE MY CURRENT BELIEFS ABOUT CREATIVITY? DRAW ONE OR MORE CARDS TO ANSWER THIS QUESTION. YOU'LL KNOW WHEN YOU'RE DONE.

DAY 2

FOR EACH BELIEF YOU UNCOVERED, DRAW ONE CARD.
WHERE DOES THIS BELIEF COME FROM?

DAY 3

WHICH OF THESE BELIEFS DON'T SERVE YOU (ANYMORE)? FOR EACH OF THEM, DRAW A CARD, ASKING 'WHY DO I HOLD ON TO THIS BELIEF?'

DAY 4

FOR EACH BELIEF THAT NO LONGER SERVES YOU, DRAW A CARD, ASKING 'WHAT DO I HAVE TO GAIN FROM LETTING THIS BELIEF GO?'

DAY 5

TAKING THIS TO HEART (CARD 1), I LET GO OF (CARD 2), SO THAT I CAN (CARD 3).

DAY 6

WHAT IS CURRENTLY MY BIGGEST ROADBLOCK WHEN IT COMES TO MY CREATIVE PROCESS?

DAY 7

WHAT AM I NOT SEEING ABOUT THIS OBSTACLE?

DAY 8

WHAT IS THIS OBSTACLE TRYING TO TEACH ME?

DAY 9

WHAT DO I NEED TO LET GO OF TO OVERCOME OR CIRCUMVENT THIS OBSTACLE?

DAY 10

WHEN IT COMES TO MY CREATIVITY, WHAT IS MY BIGGEST STRENGTH?
FEEL FREE TO DRAW MORE CARDS IF NEEDED.

DAY 11

HOW CAN I USE THIS STRENGTH (OR STRENGTHS) TO OVERCOME OR CIRCUMVENT THIS OBSTACLE?

DAY 12

WHAT IS MY BIGGEST WEAKNESS WHEN IT COMES TO MY CREATIVITY?
IF YOU FEEL THE NEED TO DRAW MORE THAN ONE CARD, DON'T DRAW MORE THAN THREE.

DAY 13

HOW DOES THIS WEAKNESS (OR WEAKNESSES) KEEP SETTING ME UP FOR FAILURE?

DAY 14

HOW CAN I TURN THIS WEAKNESS (OR THESE WEAKNESSES) INTO A STRENGTH?

DAY 15

IN WHAT WAY COULD MY STRENGTH(S) KEEP ME MORE ACCOUNTABLE?

DAY 16

WHAT DOES MY SOUL CALL ME TO CREATE RIGHT NOW?

DAY 17

WHAT DO I NEED TO KNOW ABOUT THIS DESIRE?

DAY 18

WHAT LIMITING BELIEFS DO I HAVE ABOUT THIS PARTICULAR PROJECT?

DAY 19

WHAT IS KEEPING ME FROM POURING MY HEART AND SOUL INTO THIS PROJECT?
DRAW AS MANY CARDS AS YOU NEED TO DETERMINE YOUR ROADBLOCKS.

DAY 20

FOR EACH ROADBLOCK YOU DISCOVERED, DRAW ONE CARD: WHAT AM I NOT SEEING ABOUT THIS OBSTACLE?

DAY 21

FOR EACH ROADBLOCK YOU DISCOVERED, DRAW ONE CARD: WHAT IS THIS OBSTACLE TRYING TO TEACH ME?

DAY 22

FOR EACH ROADBLOCK YOU DISCOVERED, DRAW ONE CARD: WHAT DO I NEED TO LET GO OF TO OVERCOME/CIRCUMVENT THIS OBSTACLE?

DAY 23

MY BIGGEST WEAKNESS IN RELATION TO THIS PROJECT IS (CARD 1) AND THIS (CARD 2) IS HOW IT COULD SET ME UP FOR FAILURE.

DAY 24

HOW CAN I TURN THIS WEAKNESS INTO A STRENGTH?

DAY 25

MY BIGGEST STRENGTH IN RELATION TO THIS PROJECT IS (CARD 1) AND I WILL USE IT THIS WAY (CARD 2) TO OVERCOME OR CIRCUMVENT THESE OBSTACLES.

DAY 26

HOW CAN THIS STRENGTH KEEP ME ACCOUNTABLE?

DAY 27

DRAW ONE OR MORE CARDS, ASKING 'HOW WILL THIS PROJECT FEED MY SOUL?'

DAY 28

DRAW ONE OR MORE CARDS, ASKING 'HOW WILL FINISHING THIS PROJECT FEED THE SOULS OF OTHERS?'

DAY 29

I COMMIT MYSELF TO THIS PROJECT BECAUSE (CARD 1).
I WILL KEEP MYSELF ACCOUNTABLE BY (CARD 2).

DAY 30

**WHEN I GET IN MY OWN WAY, I WILL (CARD 1)
SO THAT I CAN (CARD 2).**

DAY 31

FROM THIS DAY ON, THIS IS WHAT I WILL REMEMBER ABOUT MY CREATIVITY AND CREATIVE PROCESS.

A QUICK FAVOUR

I HOPE THIS BOOK BROUGHT YOU EVERYTHING YOU NEEDED.

IF YOU LIKED IT AND IT WAS IN ANY WAY HELPFUL, CAN I ASK YOU FOR A QUICK FAVOUR?

AUTHORS ARE NOWHERE WITHOUT HONEST REVIEWS, AND I'D TRULY APPRECIATE IT IF YOU LEFT ONE ON AMAZON, GOODREADS, OR MY FACEBOOK PAGE FACEBOOK.COM/MSWORDSMITH.

CONTACT

THERE ARE DIFFERENT WAYS AND PLACES TO FOLLOW AND CONTACT ME:

INSTAGRAM: INSTAGRAM.COM/MARIELLESSMITH
FACEBOOK: FACEBOOK.COM/MSWORDSMITH
WEBSITE: MSWORDSMITH.NL
E-MAIL: MARIELLE@MSWORDSMITH.NL

TO RECEIVE UPDATES AND STAY IN THE LOOP, SIGN UP TO MY NEWSLETTER AND GET A FREE 3-DAY EXERCISE TO OVERCOME LIMITING BELIEFS:

EEPURL.COM/DVCQKX

OTHER BOOKS BY ME

Available on Amazon and Kindle Unlimited

https://www.amazon.com/dp/B07WSGQRPS

I didn't have a specific project in mind when I picked up this book, but there are plenty of spreads that give practical advice for current works. What I did use are the spreads for getting in touch with the what you are called to create, getting in touch with the Muse, creative blocks - the big Artist's Spread at the end of the book really gave me a new perspective.

Even though you can dip in and out with each numbered spread, this book really guides you on a journey from discovering what you want to create, what might stand in your way, troubleshooting the project, and moving on to your next work.

I used both tarot and oracle cards, and got great readings with both. I'm a writer, but this book would be great for all types of creatives; it's about connecting with your intuition.

Michelle M on Amazon

OTHER BOOKS BY ME

Available on Amazon and Kindle Unlimited

https://www.amazon.com/dp/B07ZDKR8MY

Fleshing Out the Narrative: A 31-Day Tarot and Journal Challenge for Writers is designed to help you more fully understand: your story and characters; the most important story elements at play in your work; how these elements interact; and how they can best move the story forward.

Fleshing Out the Narrative walks you through 31 days of questions that will help you investigate: the premise, the theme, the hook, the setting, the main character, the antagonist, the confidant(e), the foil, and the mentor.

If you could use some divinatory help developing and expanding on your outline and story ideas, this is the book for you, whether you're into tarot, oracle, or angel cards, crystals, runes, or prefer to journal.

ACKNOWLEDGEMENTS

I'D LIKE TO THANK

SÌNE MÀIRI FOR HAVING FAITH IN ME ALWAYS

ANDRI FOR DOING THIS WITH ME

YIOTA FOR HELPING OUT WITH THE IMAGES

KAT FOR NOT MINDING SHE'S IN SOME OF THE PICTURES

MY FOLLOWERS FOR THEIR SUPPORT, ESPECIALLY THE ONES WHO PARTOOK IN THE ORIGINAL CHALLENGE

Made in the USA
Coppell, TX
27 January 2020